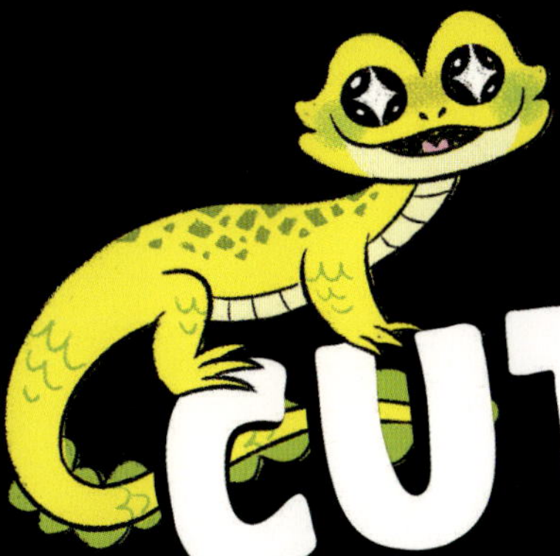

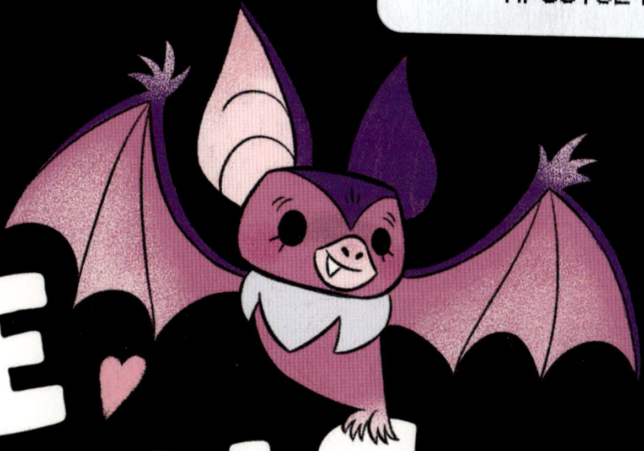

CUTE ANIMALS THAT COULD KILL YOU DEAD

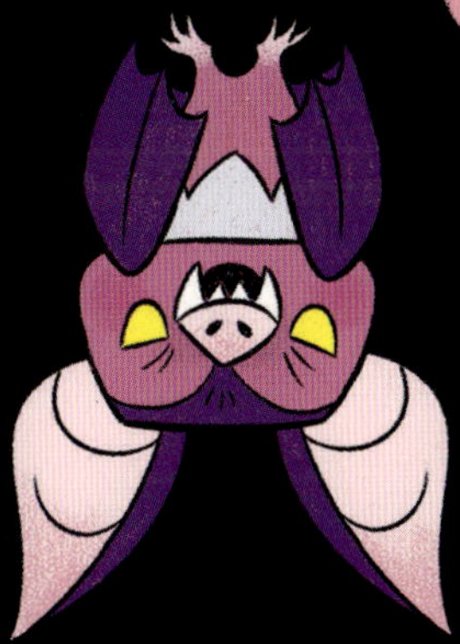

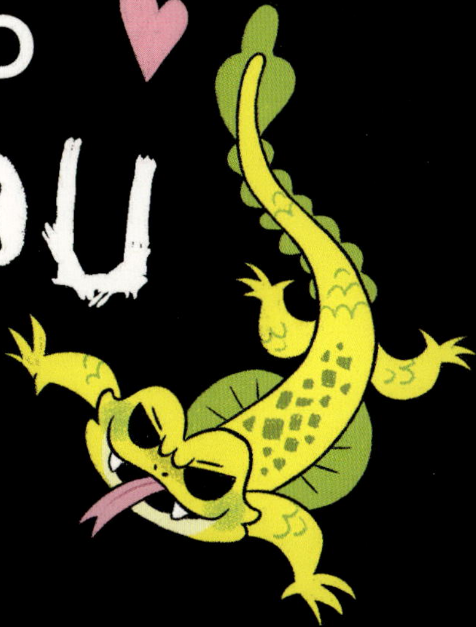

sourcebooks eXplore

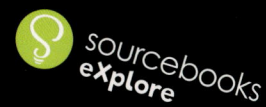

Words by **Brooke Hartman**
Pictures by **María García**

What's the first thing that comes to mind when you see a cute, cuddly face; big, gentle eyes; or soft, fuzzy paws?

QUICK, RUN AWAY!!

That wasn't what you were thinking? Well, it should be, because these seemingly sweet creatures are ready to slay…and we don't mean with their charming personalities.

Venomous spikes? Check.

Super speed? Check.

Razor-sharp claws and teeth?? Double check!

From the tops of the trees to the bottom of the ocean, from winged wonders to mighty mammals, these precious-looking predators pack a powerful punch! So lace up your running-away shoes and prepare to turn your squee into screams as we reveal the lethal-yet-lovable side of cute creatures that could kill you dead (or at least knock your socks off)!

PRECIOUS PRIMATES
TARSIER

Those sweet little feet, that bitty button nose, and those wide, adorable eyes...that are watching your every move! At first glance, tarsiers might seem like dainty darlings, but these pint-size primates are master hunters.

SCIENTIFIC NAME: Tarsiidae
SIZE: 4–6 inches (10–15 cm) tall
HABITAT: Southeast Asia
FAVOURITE FOOD: Insects, lizards, and snakes
CONSERVATION STATUS: Most tarsier species are endangered or threatened. Their numbers have dwindled significantly from habitat destruction, hunting, pollution, and human disturbance.

AWW-DORABLE LEVEL
AAAAH!-SOME LEVEL

"EYE SEE YOU!"

Tarsiers are carnivores and will stalk any potential meal, including insects, lizards, and even **VENOMOUS SNAKES**! Their unique rugby-ball-shaped head helps keep those enormous eyes perfectly still while they wait for prey. A tarsier can even swivel its head like an owl to track down dinner, and their ears are shaped like satellite dishes, allowing them to hear extremely high frequencies so they know when a tasty tidbit is nearby.

Once a meal is spotted, they use their **STRONG HIND LEGS** to leap up to fifteen feet (about 4.5 kilometres) and land directly on their prey, which they snatch up with their large hands. Now that's a snack attack!

PRECIOUS PRIMATES
SLOW LORIS

Here's a face that will make you scream... "Cuddle me," that is! With their large, gentle eyes, teensy ears, and fluffy fur, the slow loris would look right at home in your stuffed toy collection. Their adorable level is so high, they can turn that cute factor right on its head: they have special toes for hanging on to branches for hours at a time, even upside down!

SCIENTIFIC NAME: *Nycticebus*
SIZE: 7.1–15 inches (18–38 cm) tall
HABITAT: Southeast Asia
FAVOURITE FOOD: Fruit
CONSERVATION STATUS: Most species of slow loris are listed as either vulnerable or endangered. Their numbers are threatened by illegal hunting and capturing and habitat loss.

AWW-DORABLE LEVEL
AAAAH!-SOME LEVEL

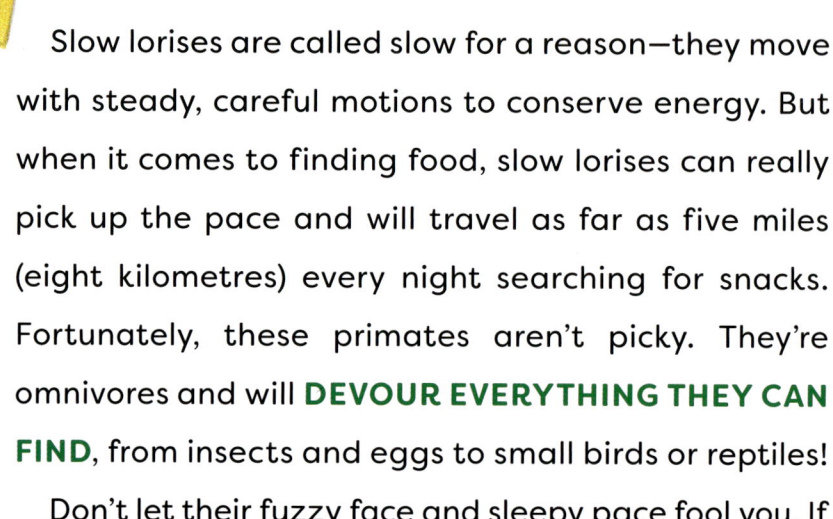

Slow lorises are called slow for a reason—they move with steady, careful motions to conserve energy. But when it comes to finding food, slow lorises can really pick up the pace and will travel as far as five miles (eight kilometres) every night searching for snacks. Fortunately, these primates aren't picky. They're omnivores and will **DEVOUR EVERYTHING THEY CAN FIND**, from insects and eggs to small birds or reptiles! Don't let their fuzzy face and sleepy pace fool you. If cornered or attacked, slow lorises have a surprise up their sleeve—literally. When faced with a predator, they will lick a gland on their upper arm that contains toxins, then lick those toxins all over their body, resulting in **POISONOUS FUR** and a venomous bite. Slow lorises are the **ONLY VENOMOUS PRIMATE IN THE WORLD**! Their toxin is similar to what causes allergies to animal fur, but it's strong enough to make your skin rot like a zombie! If you were bitten, it would really be *horror-fying*.

"I GIVE PREDATORS A GOOD LICKING!"

NIBBLE, NIBBLE, LITTLE CRITTER

GRASSHOPPER MOUSE

How can anyone not go gaga for grasshopper mice, with their wee whiskery noses, big bright eyes, and itty-bitty bodies that would fit in the palm of your hand? But that's the last place you'd want them to be!

SCIENTIFIC NAME: *Onychomys*
SIZE: 3.5–5 inches (8.9–12.7 cm) long
HABITAT: North America (Southern United States and Mexico)
FAVOURITE FOOD: Scorpions
CONSERVATION STATUS: Some species of grasshopper mice are listed as a species of concern, with numbers declining due to habitat loss.

AWW-DORABLE LEVEL
AAAAH!-SOME LEVEL

These pocket-size rodents might be as small as a pine cone, but when it comes to hunting, **THEY'RE NO PIPSQUEAKS**. Their skulls and teeth resemble those of larger carnivores, such as cats and dogs. But a grasshopper mouse's bite is much worse than its bark. These minuscule hunters are highly aggressive and can bite the heads off their meals with one nip of their long front teeth. Grasshopper mice will also take down prey much larger—and more deadly—than themselves, such as tarantulas, centipedes, and small venomous snakes.

But their absolute favourite food? **SCORPIONS**. Grasshopper mice love these succulent snacks so much, they've adapted to withstand scorpion venom. They can even turn the venom into medicine to dull pain, so the more a grasshopper mouse gets stung, the less it gets hurt! When a grasshopper mouse nabs a meal, it throws back its head and lets out a high-pitched howl, giving it the nickname "werewolf mouse." Now that's *howl-arious*!

"WE HAVE A HOWLING GOOD TIME. HOWOOOOOOOO!"

NIBBLE, NIBBLE, LITTLE CRITTER

HEDGEHOG

Look in the dictionary under "adorable" and you'll probably find this furry face peeking back at you. With their plump, prickly bodies and sniffly snouts, these precious pincushions are in a cuteness class all their own! Don't let that furry face fool you, though—hedgehogs are built for battle!

SCIENTIFIC NAME: *Erinaceus*

SIZE: 4–12 inches (10–30 cm) long

HABITAT: As their name suggests, hedgehogs often live near hedges, but they also love pasturelands, gardens, deserts, woodlands, and even urban backyards across Europe, Asia, Africa, and New Zealand.

FAVOURITE FOOD: Anything from roots and mushrooms to bugs, eggs, and small reptiles!

CONSERVATION STATUS: Hedgehogs aren't considered endangered at this point, but wild populations of hedgehogs in Europe have been recently declining.

AWW-DORABLE LEVEL

AAAAH!-SOME LEVEL

When hedgehogs are threatened, they curl up in a tight, prickly ball with as many as **SIX THOUSAND QUILLS**. That's a lot of pokes! Hedgehogs will sometimes add extra protection by munching on toxic plants, then licking that toxin onto their spines to add even more ouch to any possible predators.

But hedgehogs aren't just good at avoiding predators—they're excellent predators themselves. Every night, hedgehogs go hog wild and roam over a mile (two kilometres) in search of supper. Those tiny tootsies might seem adorable, but they each have **FIVE RAZOR CLAWS** that let them run, dig, swim, and climb trees to grab some grub—or grubs!

And that sweet face is hiding a not-so-sweet surprise: **FORTY-FOUR SHARP TEETH**! So when they track down a tasty treat, they have no problem snatching it up and gobbling it down. Hedgehogs can devour up to a third of their body weight each night! Fortunately, hedgehogs aren't picky. They'll chomp down anything from plants to insects, mice, eggs, birds, and reptiles. They even munch venomous centipedes and wasps, whose stings don't seem to bother them at all. No matter the meal, these prickly pals really pig out!

"WE DO THE HOGGY-POKEY AND WE STICK OUR PRICKLES OUT... THAT'S WHAT IT'S ALL ABOUT!"

WEENSY WINGERS

NORTHERN PYGMY OWL

AWW-DORABLE LEVEL

AAAAH!-SOME LEVEL

What do you get when you mix two wide, round eyes with two ounces of feathery floof? The northern pygmy owl! Weighing no more than a golf ball, this is one itty-bitty birdy. But while the pygmy owl might be petite, it's 100 percent predator!

SCIENTIFIC NAME: *Glaucidium californicum*
SIZE: 6–7 inches (15–17 cm) long
HABITAT: Forests of North America
FAVOURITE FOOD: Rodents and other birds
CONSERVATION STATUS: Not threatened with no evidence of decline

These tiny raptors are in a fierceness class *owl* their own and gobble up more critters than other larger birds of prey. For a pygmy owl, **ALMOST ANYTHING IS ON THE MENU** from insects, mice, and (gulp!) other backyard birdies! They'll even hunt down animals three times their size, such as squirrels or gophers. That would be like chasing a moose for supper every night!

Unlike many other owls, the northern pygmy owl is diurnal and prefers to hunt at dawn and dusk, but these brutal birds won't hesitate to snag an afternoon or even midnight snack. When they catch extra food, pygmy owls often hang it in trees or on thorns, the same way you might keep your treats in a refrigerator. How *cool* is that?

You might have heard the saying that owls have eyes on the backs of their heads, but the pygmy owl takes this one feather further. The backs of their heads have bright yellow feathers that look just like eye spots, possibly to warn any other nearby critters that **THIS OWL'S GOT THEIR EYE ON YOU**. But one thing's certain: the pygmy owl is one *owl*-some bird!

"WHOOOO DRANK ALL THE BEETLE JUICE?"

WEENSY WINGERS

BUMBLEBEE BAT
(KITTI'S HOG-NOSED BAT)

It's a bird! It's a bumblebee! It's cuter than both of those put together! It's an itsy-bitsy, teensy-weensy, super sweet...bat?

AWW-DORABLE LEVEL

AAAAH!-SOME LEVEL

SCIENTIFIC NAME: *Craseonycteris thonglongyai*

SIZE: 1–1.3 inches (29–33 mm) long (*Wow that's tiny!*)

HABITAT: Limestone caves near rivers in Thailand and Myanmar

FAVOURITE FOOD: Flies

CONSERVATION STATUS: The Thailand population may be at risk of extinction due to habitat loss from burning of forests and human disturbance of roosting sites.

"CARE FOR AN IN-FLIGHT SNACK?"

At no bigger than your thumb, the bumblebee bat is the most minuscule mammal in the world. These bitty beasties only grow to about one inch long (about 2.5 centimetres) and weigh less than 0.1 ounce (two grams). That's no bigger than a penny! Despite their munchkin status, bumblebee bats are packed with predator prowess and only need to leave their caves to hunt for less than an hour every night. But in that short amount of time, these hog-nosed bats really pork out, gobbling as many as **FOUR THOUSAND INSECTS**. That's a lot of bug bites!

How do they snatch all those insect snacks? With a mix of **SUPERSONIC SOUND AND SOARING STEALTH**! Using echolocation, bumblebee bats will screech up to 220 times every second, then listen for the echo to bounce off their bug breakfast. Bumblebee bats' wings are long and wide—as long as five times the length of their bodies! Using those extra-long wings, bumblebee bats will chase, soar, and dive after their dinner, seeking spiders, beetles, and other insects clinging to leaves and tree trunks. But their favourite meal is anything they catch while flying, which might be why their favourite snack is...flies!

WATER BABIES
SEA OTTER

Can you think of a friendlier face on land or water than the playful, paddly otter? Or maybe we should say, *aww-ter!* Most people know otters for their curiosity and fun personalities, right? Wrong!

SCIENTIFIC NAME: *Enhydra lutris*

SIZE: Ranging between species, 2–5.9 feet (0.6–1.8 m) long

HABITAT: Oceans around all continents except Australia and Antarctica

FAVOURITE FOODS: Shellfish and fish

CONSERVATION STATUS: Some otter species in California and Alaska are listed as threatened. All otters are protected under the Marine Mammal Protection Act.

COME ON, IT'S AN OTTER!

AWW-DORABLE LEVEL

AAAAH!-SOME LEVEL

Well, wrong for all the fish, frogs, turtles, insects, and small mammals that make up an otter's meals. Large male sea otters devour as much as twenty-five pounds (about eleven kilograms) of food each day. That's more than fifty tuna sandwiches!

But snatching all those delicious fish dishes is easy when you're **100 PERCENT PREDATOR**. Sea otters have a ton of *otter-ly* awesome hunting traits such as speed, stealth, and smarts. They're like furry underwater ninjas! Using the force of their powerful flippers, otters can dive up to 250 feet (76 metres) below the surface where they use their whiskers, or vibrissae, to sense prey's movement through the water. Otters also have a large lung capacity, over two and a half times more than other animals their size. These jumbo lungs help an otter stay underwater for as long as eight minutes to seek a deep-sea dinner. But once a seafood snack is spotted—watch out! That toothy otter grin has **THIRTY-SIX SHARP TEETH** made for chomping. Otters even keep a stone in the fur beneath their arm to break open clamshells. So whether they're diving for dinner or just having a *l-otter* fun, these playful predators really rock out!

"LET'S TAKE A SHELL-FIE!"

"HANG ON, LET ME GET MY CLAM-ERA."

WATER BABIES
PLATYPUS

At first glance, the platypus might look a little ridiculous. Ridiculously cute, that is! That soft fur, those waddly webbed feet, that darling duck bill, and those...venomous talons?

SCIENTIFIC NAME: *Ornithorhynchus anatinus*

SIZE: 16–24 inches (40–60 cm) long

HABITAT: From the steamy jungles of Australia to the snowy mountains of Tasmania

FAVOURITE FOODS: Shrimp, crayfish, worms, and insect larvae

CONSERVATION STATUS: Though platypus numbers have grown with conservation efforts, their populations are threatened by habitat loss and creek damming, and they are listed as an endangered species in South Australia.

AWW-DORABLE LEVEL

AAAAH!-SOME LEVEL

"HOW MANY WAYS CAN A PLATYPUS FIND FOOD?"

That's right, both male and female platypuses have venomous barbs on their back ankles. The barbs on a male platypus contain venom so powerful, it's **LETHAL** to small animals. Like medieval knights, platypuses only use their barbs when battling other platypuses for a mate, but it's still nothing to joust about. If you were to get accidentally poked by one, the venom feels like hundreds of hornets stinging at once. Yeowch!

Platypuses are **NOCTURNAL** and spend over twelve hours every night searching for snacks. That's a long lunchtime! In that time, platypuses munch more than one-fifth of their body weight, gulping down shrimp, crayfish, worms, and insect larvae. Good thing these plucky predators have so many traits to help them hunt. A platypus's webbed front feet make excellent paddles, propelling them fast through the water, while their hind legs and beaver-like tail act as rudders to steer. Even the platypus's bill is more than just ducky—its outer skin contains special nerves that help scan murky water for prey, like a **BUILT-IN DINNER DETECTOR**. So when it comes to hunting, a platypus really fits the bill!

"ABOUT A BILL-ION!"

BABY BUGGIES
LADYBIRD

With their round, rosy bodies and polka-dot spots, ladybirds are one of the cutest critters on the planet. Not only are they absolutely adorable, they're also thought to be good luck. In fact, many people make a wish when they see a ladybird. And if you were an aphid, you'd be wishing all right...wishing to make a quick getaway!

SCIENTIFIC NAME: Coccinellidae
SIZE: 0.3–0.4 inches (0.75–1 cm) long
HABITAT: Europe and North America
FAVOURITE FOOD: Aphids and aphid larvae
CONSERVATION STATUS: Ladybird populations are threatened by climate change, light pollution, and pesticide use worldwide.

AWW-DORABLE LEVEL
AAAAH!-SOME LEVEL

Ladybirds are hunting machines; each one of these bitsy beetles can gobble as many as **SIXTY APHIDS A DAY**. That's over twenty thousand aphid appetisers a year! Ladybirds don't see well, but that doesn't stop these puny predators from devouring every bad bug for miles. Ladybirds have a strong sense of smell and powerful jaws. When sniffing out an aphid snack, ladybirds use those jaws to snatch, smash, and slice their prey into bite-size bits. **EVEN LADYBIRD LARVAE ARE DEADLY**—they start hunting right after they hatch and can chomp through over two hundred aphids a week. Those are some hungry babies!

"WHY AREN'T LADYBIRDS GOOD AT HIDE AND SEEK?"

"THEY'RE USUALLY SPOTTED!"

Although a ladybird's cheerful hue might look adorable to you, predators wouldn't agree. Bright colours signal that ladybird are no savoury snack. When ladybirds are attacked, they release a smelly substance on their legs that makes them taste awful. But one thing's for sure, having ladybirds around makes a lot of *scents*.

BABY BUGGIES

JUMPING SPIDER

At no bigger than your fingernail, jumping spiders take itsy-bitsy spider to a whole new level. But who can resist that tiny spidey face? Nobody, including all the crickets, flies, roaches, mealworms, moths, and even small frogs and lizards that end up as a jumping spider's snacks.

SCIENTIFIC NAME: Salticidae
SIZE: 0.24–0.59 inches (6–15 mm) long
HABITAT: Tropical and temperate forests, mountain regions, scrublands, and deserts worldwide
FAVOURITE FOODS: Insects, small frogs, and lizards
CONSERVATION STATUS: Not threatened, though pollution and deforestation may reduce habitat

AWW-DORABLE LEVEL
AAAAH!-SOME LEVEL

Jumping spiders may be small, but these puny predators are super hunters. Those beady eyes aren't just cute, they give jumping spiders **BINOCULAR VISION** and provide a wide range of colour detail. Their eyes can also swivel, allowing the spider to look around without moving a muscle. And though they don't have ears, jumping spiders are wired for sound: tiny hairs on their bodies take in vibrations and send those signals directly to the spiders' brains, making their entire bug body a mini satellite dish!

Jumping spiders also have super spider smarts. One jumping spider named Kim was trained by researchers to jump on command! Of course, they're called jumping spiders for a reason. Their little back legs have a **HYDRAULIC SYSTEM** like what bulldozers use for heavy lifting. When a jumping spider wants to leap, it uses special muscles to increase blood flow to its legs. This enables them to jump as far as fifty times the length of their bodies! They can also spin webbing like a bungee cord to swing down onto unsuspecting meals. Talk about dropping in for a quick bite!

"I ALWAYS JUMP TO CONCLUSIONS!"

DEEP BLUE SQUEE!

BOTTLENOSE DOLPHIN

With their sweet smiles and cheerful chirps, bottlenose dolphins are one of the cutest creatures on the planet. But those cheerful chirps can be used as **ECHOLOCATION** to seek out their next meal, and those sweet smiles hide a sinister side...

SCIENTIFIC NAME: *Tursiops truncatus*
SIZE: 6–13 feet (2–4 m) long
HABITAT: Temperate and tropical waters worldwide
FAVOURITE FOODS: Fish, shrimp, crabs, and squid
CONSERVATION STATUS: Bottlenose dolphins are not threatened, but they are protected under the Marine Mammal Protection Act.

AWW-DORABLE LEVEL
AAAAH!-SOME LEVEL

...up to one hundred **SHARP TEETH**!

When it comes to hunting, these marine mammals are no flukes and can gobble up to thirty pounds (13.6 kilograms) of fish, squid, shrimp, and crabs a day! To nab all those deep-sea dinners, bottlenose dolphins use a **LETHAL MIX OF TEAMWORK, SPEED, AND SUPER SMARTS**. They're considered the second most intelligent animal on Earth and easily outwit potential prey by hunting in packs, cooperating to circle schools of fish, then taking turns to dive in and feed. And those dives are deep; scientists once observed a dolphin diving 1,280 feet (390 metres) for a meal. That's as high as a ten-storey building! They also have special circulatory systems that can slow down their heart rate and breathing to conserve oxygen. This allows dolphins to prowl beneath the waves for up to twenty minutes before they have to surface for air. Talk about a deep breath!

Bottlenose dolphins will also slap their tails on water to scare fish out of hiding places or stun fish by flipping them into the air, like a fresh fish flapjack. So whether they're splashing for fun or *on porpoise*, a dolphin can really flip out!

"WE'RE SIMPLY STUNNING!"

DEEP BLUE SQUEE!
SEA BUNNY

AWW-DORABLE LEVEL

AAAAH!-SOME LEVEL

What's not to love about a tiny fluffy bunny that lives in the ocean? Maybe the fact that it's also...

SCIENTIFIC NAME: *Jorunna parva*
SIZE: 0.98 inches (2.5 cm) long
HABITAT: Oceans surrounding Asia and Australia
FAVOURITE FOOD: Sea sponges
CONSERVATION STATUS: Unknown. Sea bunny and sea slug numbers are hard to determine but may be declining due to pollution and loss of coral reefs.

...a **TOXIC CARNIVORE**!

These bonny wee bun buns are actually a type of sea slug. Their "ears," called rhinophores, act like noses that help search the sea for snacks. And all that fluff is really papillae, which are sensory organs like the taste buds on your tongue. That means sea bunnies are constantly tasting the water around them to see if it contains something yummy. Imagine licking everything in your house to see if it might be food!

"NO TOUCHY!"

While sea bunnies aren't fast (you could say they're a little sluggish), any animal that tries to have a sea bunny for a meal is in for a shock. These sweet sea slugs snack on sea sponges (say that three times fast), and those sponges contain toxins that **SEA BUNNIES CONVERT TO POISON IN THEIR SKIN**. It might not be strong enough to seriously injure a person, but it still packs a powerful punch. So resist the urge to pet that fluffy head!

COLD-BLOODED CUTIES

POISON DART FROG

AWW-DORABLE LEVEL

AAAAH!-SOME LEVEL

These adorable amphibians look like they hopped right off a rainbow. Unfortunately, those flashy hues won't lead you to a pot of gold.

SCIENTIFIC NAME: Dendrobatidae

SIZE: 0.59–2.4 inches (1.5–6 cm) long

HABITAT: Central and South America

FAVOURITE FOODS: Ants, mites, flies, and termites

CONSERVATION STATUS: Many species are listed as endangered or critically endangered; climate change and habitat loss threaten their survival.

Instead, these puny frogs pack a poisonous pow!

A poison dart frog's bright colours are a signal like a stop sign to predators, warning them to **STAY AWAY**—and for good reason. Poison dart frogs build up poison in their skin from toxins in the insects they eat. And though each little bug doesn't have much toxin, poison dart frogs devour as many as seventy-five insects a day! Munching all that poison really adds up; each little froggy contains **ENOUGH TOXIN TO KILL UP TO TEN THOUSAND MICE**. Now that's a lot of croaking!

How about this *ribbet-ing* fact: to get all those juicy bugs, poison dart frogs use their keen vision to spot prey. When they spy a delicious insect dish, their long, sticky tongue darts out and slurps up the snack. Then the tongue rolls back into the frog's mouth, ready to strike again. A poison dart frog's favourite foods are ants, mites, flies, and termites, but they'll bite just about anything that bugs them. Just make sure it isn't you!

"I'D LIKE A LARGE FLIES AND A DIET CROAK."

COLD-BLOODED CUTIES

FLYING GECKO

What animal has two button eyes, a great big grin...and is a cold-blooded, stealth-swooping, night ninja? The flying gecko of course! These agile amphibians might be good little geckos who eat their veggies, but for the most part, these cute characters are mostly carnivores! Smaller flying geckos munch on worms, snails, and other insects. But the bigger the gecko, the bigger the gulp!

SCIENTIFIC NAME: *Ptychozoon kuhli*
SIZE: 4-8 inches (10-20 cm) long
HABITAT: Jungles of southeast Asia
FAVOURITE FOODS: Fruit and nectar, insects, worms, snails, and small lizards and snakes
CONSERVATION STATUS: Though their species is not currently threatened, flying geckos are considered rare in their natural habitat.

AWW-DORABLE LEVEL
AAAAH!-SOME LEVEL

Larger flying geckos will eat small salamanders, other lizards, and even snakes! If you're a potential snack, you'd better watch your back; the flying gecko can glide up to **TWO HUNDRED FEET** (about 61 metres) from tree to tree using flaps of skin on their feet and tails. Now that's a sight for *soar*-ing eyes! Speaking of sight, geckos have eyes that are 350 times more sensitive to light than a human's. This allows them to pick out colours, shapes, and movements even in dim light—like watching colour TV in the dark!

"WE'RE AIR-MAZING!"

Like all geckos, flying geckos are able to drop their tails when being chased by a predator. You read that right—when a gecko gets grabbed, **ITS TAIL COMES *OFF*** and continues to twitch and thrash, causing a distraction that allows the gecko to escape! If you thought that *tail* was cool, check out this gripping fact: geckos can cling to surfaces upside-down, even metal or glass! With such a neat feat (or *feet*?), you'd think their toes were covered with glue, but they're actually covered in tiny hairs called setae—over sixty-five million setae, in fact, which is enough sticking force to support the weight of four kids! Good thing geckos don't have kid on the menu! So whether escaping predators or leaping after lunch, these *toe-tally* awesome geckos soar through any sticky situations!

FUZZY AND FUR-OCIOUS

BLACK-FOOTED CAT

This itty-bitty kitty is *paw*-sitively one of the cutest cats around! Barely bigger than a football and weighing no more than a can of soup, the black-footed cat looks like it would be quite comfortable curled up at the foot of your bed. But don't let its pint size fool you...

SCIENTIFIC NAME: *Felis nigripes*
SIZE: 14–20 inches (35–52 cm) long
HABITAT: South Africa
FAVOURITE FOODS: Rodents, birds, amphibians, reptiles, insects, and spiders
CONSERVATION STATUS: Endangered; populations are declining due to poaching and habitat loss.

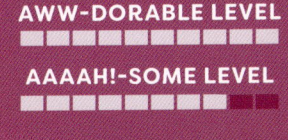

AWW-DORABLE LEVEL

AAAAH!-SOME LEVEL

"WE'RE NOT KITTEN AROUND!"

This furry little feline is the **DEADLIEST CAT ON EARTH**!

Their high metabolism means they're always on the lookout for their next meal, so it's a good thing these cuddly cats are also prey-catching powerhouses.

Black-footed cats are all carnivore and will chow down on everything from insects and reptiles to rodents and birds. They'll also go after much larger prey than themselves, such as hares. Basically, if it's made out of meat, it's good for them to eat! Black-footed cats can leap almost **FIVE FEET HIGH** (around 1.5 metres) and will snatch birds right out of the air, but they can also be sneaky, weaving slowly through brush or waiting near burrows to pounce on unsuspecting meals. This combination of swiftness and stealth makes them the purr-fect hunters!

FUZZY AND FUR-OCIOUS

FENNEC FOX

AWW-DORABLE LEVEL

AAAAH!-SOME LEVEL

With two huge ears and a goofy grin, fennec foxes look more like a cartoon character than a real animal. But fennec foxes aren't just fur-real.

SCIENTIFIC NAME: *Vulpes zerda*

SIZE: Head and body: 9.5–16 inches (24–40 cm); tail: 7–12.2 inches (18–31 cm)

HABITAT: Deserts of North Africa, Sinai, and the Arabian peninsula

FAVOURITE FOODS: Plants and roots to eggs, insects, reptiles, small birds, rodents, and rabbits

CONSERVATION STATUS: Fennec foxes are currently listed as a status of least concern and are not endangered, but their populations are still threatened due to the pet and fur trade, habitat loss, and climate change.

They're also fur-ocious! These fuzzy-but-fierce foxes are omnivores, which means just about anything is on the menu from plants to eggs, insects, reptiles, birds, and rodents. They definitely aren't *fennec-ky* eaters!

That fluffy coat and bushy tail might make it appear as though they're ready for a snow day, but fennec foxes are desert dwellers. Though they make their homes beneath the sizzling sun, they prefer to come out at dusk when the dunes become an all-night diner.

Fennec foxes use their big ears like satellite dishes to listen for underground prey. When they hear a midnight snack, they use their padded paws to dig, dig, dig to where the prey might be hiding. And if their dinner tries to make a dash for it—**WATCH OUT**! A fennec fox's furry paw "boots" give them extra traction to run fast across the sand. Now that's a fox-trot! And those bitty bodies pack some serious muscle. Fennec foxes can jump **TWO FEET** (0.6 metres) high from a standing position and leap a distance of **FOUR FEET** (1.2 metres). That's a lot of pounce per ounce!

"WHEN IT COMES TO FINDING FOOD, WE'RE ALL EARS!"

FUZZY AND FUR-OCIOUS
HONEY BADGER

An adorable face wrapped in soft, dark fur and coated with a white, sugary stripe—what's not to love about the honey badger? But despite the name, these cute critters aren't known for their sweet personality.

SCIENTIFIC NAME: *Mellivora capensis*

SIZE: 22–30 inches (55–77 cm) long

HABITAT: Africa, Southwest Asia, and India

FAVOURITE FOOD: Insects, amphibians, reptiles, birds, mammals, roots, plants, fruits, and of course—honey!

CONSERVATION STATUS: Though widespread and abundant, honey badgers are listed as endangered in some areas due to overhunting.

AWW-DORABLE LEVEL

AAAAH!-SOME LEVEL

"HOW SWEET OF YOU!"

Honey badgers are known as the **WORLD'S MOST FEARLESS ANIMAL**, and for good reason! A honey badger's bite is super strong, which comes in handy since they chomp down almost everything: roots, eggs, insects, frogs, lizards, birds, and—you guessed it—honey. To get this sweet treat, honey badgers emit a smell that's so suffocating, it chases bees away from their hives. They can also release the smell when cornered, **STINK BOMB STYLE**. What a *scents* of humour!

If a honey badger is attacked, it will fight viciously with its strong, sharp claws and can even fend off much larger animals such as hyenas and lions. Their skin is so thick that bee stings, porcupine quills, and animal bites barely hurt them. Honey badgers are highly intelligent; they'll use tools to get a hard-to-reach meal and will work together to escape from pens. One famous honey badger named Stoffel escaped from his pen at a wildlife sanctuary over a dozen times! But the biggest reason honey badgers make the list of killer cuties? They love to snack on highly venomous snakes like cobras and black mambas. Good thing **THEY'RE RESISTANT TO VENOM**, because that breakfast bites back!

ABOUT THE AUTHOR

Brooke Hartman is an award-winning author of silly, serious, and sometimes strange books for kids. Born and raised in the wild state of Alaska, she knows all about cute, furry animals that would love for you pet them—so they can have you for dinner. Although she grew up wishing she was a unicorn, she now wishes she were a dragon so she could roast marshmallows with her fiery breath. She and her family live at the base of Alaska's Chugach Mountains, along with a guinea pig who openly plots to eat all the vegetables in the universe, and a chocolate Lab who believes all passing cars are driven by velociraptors.

ABOUT THE ILLUSTRATOR

María García was born and raised in the not-so-wild city of Seville, Spain. Growing up in a pack of artists, she was able to find her own knack for the arts from a young age. But as she grew up, she ventured beyond the trees of her jungle and trained as a designer and illustrator. Though she's a harmless human, she wishes she had spider legs so she could illustrate several stories at once and swing from web to web from time to time. One of her dreams is to have a pet with multiple rows of teeth, capable of scaring off intruders but also of winning hearts with its sweet gaze.

To Ethan and Avery, who are adorable and AAAAAAAH!!!-some.

—Auntie Brooke

To my parents, my sister, and my partner in crime, for their huge support.

—MG

Text © 2025 by Brooke Hartman
Illustrations © 2025 by María García
Cover and internal design © 2025 by Sourcebooks
Cover and internal design by Michelle Mayhall/Sourcebooks
Internal photos © Alamy: Eng Wah Teo. Getty Images: Charoenchai Tothaisong, David McGowen, Diem Demirci / 500px, Eros 45 / 500px, eZeePics Studio, Floridapfe from S.Korea Kim in cherl, luamduan, Michel VIARD, Muhammad Owais Khan, Peter Pokrovsky, slowmotiongli, Steve Adams, Weber, Zsuzsanna Jenei. Mona Dienhart. Shutterstock: Erwin Niemand.

Sourcebooks and the colophon are registered trademarks of Sourcebooks.

All rights reserved.

All brand names and product names used in this book are trademarks, registered trademarks, or trade names of their respective holders. Sourcebooks is not associated with any product or vendor in this book.

All book illustrations have been sketched and coloured in Photoshop using an XP-Pen tablet.

Published by Sourcebooks eXplore, an imprint of Sourcebooks Kids
P.O. Box 4410, Naperville, Illinois 60567-4410
(630) 961-3900
sourcebookskids.com

Cataloging-in-Publication Data is on file with the Library of Congress.

Source of Production: 1010 Printing Asia Limited, Kwun Tong, Hong Kong, China
Date of Production: October 2024
Run Number: 5041621

Printed and bound in China.
OGP 10 9 8 7 6 5 4 3 2 1